Staying Young Growing Old

Positive Thinking and Motivational Strategies

Marji Hill

Prison Tree Press

DEDICATION

This book is dedicated to Alex Barlow (1926-2012), my partner of forty years. He is the inspiration for *Staying Young Growing Old* . On his 75th birthday he received a birthday card which read " Take on the next 25 years with energy and vigor and the production of many new enterprises."

Alex decided "Yes" that was certainly his intention. He planned the projects that he wanted to achieve and he set a timetable for their completion. This book is the result of one of those projects.

Why? Alex well knew that staying young in spirit, mind and action was important for him as time would take a toll on his body. Alex still had much to give. To stay young in ways that he could was going to help him go on giving.

If Alex could help other older people find ways to stay young too as they go on giving, then more and more people will find that growing old may carry much more pleasure for them than they imagined it ever could.

Alex's life encompassed six careers: teacher, priest, librarian, writer, sociologist and barrister. Even when he retired from formal employment at age 65 he reinvented himself by doing a law degree at the Australian National University in Canberra and was admitted to the Bar in 1995. In the course of his writing career he became an award winning author having more than 80 books published on all aspects of Indigenous Australia.

He was a great mentor and confidant to many people inspiring them to cultivate their talents and to bring the best out of their lives.

This book was Alex's vision and goal in his final years and I have completed it for him.

Table of Contents

ACKNOWLEDGMENTS

I thank my friend Sherien Foley on the Gold Coast for her friendship, endless support, and her assistance with editing the manuscript. I also thank John Foley for his encouragement in pursuing this theme, and to Blan MacDonagh in Adelaide for reading the manuscript when the project was in its infancy. My appreciation also goes to Eleanor Coombe in Tasmania for trial blazing the way and mentoring me on this publishing process.

1. INTRODUCTION

Old age is like everything else. To make a success of it, you've got to start young.
Theodore Roosevelt

"With age you can lose some of the fearlessness that you have when you are very young." These were the words of Daniel Barenboim when a television documentary about a brilliant young violinist, Maxim Vengerov showed him rehearsing with the noted conductor and pianist.

Can you remember how fearless you were when you were very young? Do you remember what you could do and what you were like when you were 8 or 10 or 12? Alex Barlow can remember the experience of running along the footpath down the hill from his home to the corner shop. "I felt as though I was flying through the evening air. I didn't think Olympics. I just knew I could run fast. Just flying. I wasn't beating anybody. It wasn't a race against someone else. Competition was something I was yet to learn. It was just the joy of running, flying fast. Being young. BEING. YOUNG. That's staying young growing old".

This is what this book is about.

2. YES YOU CAN

You can't help getting older, but you don't have to get old.
George Burns

Begin Again   At the age of 89 Cecile Dorward saw the publication of her life's story.   She called her book, *Anything But Ordinary, the Nine Lives of Cecile*.   At age 58 she left her home in Cottesloe in Western Australia and her job at the Royal Perth Hospital and began a campervan tour that over the next 26 years took her through Europe, Morocco, South Africa and overland all the way from Australia to London.   She happily picked up hitch-hikers along the way and enjoyed their company, listening to their stories over many hours.   She was 84 when she finished these journeys.   Then she began to work on her ninth 'life' as an author.

That's staying young growing old.

Dare When Dagmar Gilfelt had her eightieth birthday she made her first free fall parachute jump from 3050 metres in the skies above Australia's national capital, Canberra. She decided to make the jump while she still could. This was her birthday present to herself because she loved heights.

That's staying young growing old.

Say "Next" Jon Cleary saw his first book, a collection of short stories, published in 1946. His best known book, *The Sundowner* sold over 3 million copies. The book was made into a film in the 1960s. Cleary had more than fifty works of fiction published and sold over eight million copies throughout the world. He said he thought of retiring with his fiftieth book but then thought what he would do for therapy. He came up with a new idea and a couple of characters..."

That's staying young growing old.

Keep the Flame   She has been called "the greatest living poet of the Australian landscape", "Australia's greatest woman poet', "the greatest woman poet since Sappho", but a week before she died, just after she had been pushed in her wheelchair across the Commonwealth Bridge in Canberra's Walk for Reconciliation 2000, Judith Wright said,

"Anyone can write poetry, but to be an activist is far more important".

Judith Wright, born 1915, had inherited from her father a passion for conservation to which she later added Australian Indigenous issues.   She began writing seriously in 1942, but by the 1970s she had become one of Australia's most significant political activists. Increasingly she turned from poetry to prose as the best way to present the social and environmental issues that concerned her.   In 1993 reporter John Glover of the Sydney Morning Herald asked her why she had not stuck to poetry saying "There are so few great poets and so many activists". She replied, "But there aren't. I get poetry flooding my desk every day, most of it no good, but a really good activist..." Hearing impaired, physically handicapped, and ill, she would not miss the Reconciliation March. She kept the flame of her passion alive to the end.

That's staying young growing old.

Learn to Change There were many reasons why Malcolm Fraser, conservative Liberal Prime Minister of Australia 1975–1983, was disliked as a politician, not only by his political opponents but by members of his own Liberal constituency. In his later years Fraser supported the cause of an Australian Republic, and actively worked for Aboriginal Reconciliation. He called on the then Liberal Prime Minister, John Howard to say "sorry' to Australian Indigenous people for the many injustices inflicted on them in the past. He proposed a re-evaluation of the alliance between Australia and the United States of America.

Fraser's views came a long way from the policies he followed as Prime Minister. He admitted that the world had changed tremendously, and that he had been prepared to change his views with it. He was only 53 when he gave up his parliamentary career. Fraser confessed that the change took a lot of adjusting to.

As a former Prime Minister it was not appropriate for Fraser to continue to be involved then in Australian issues, so he welcomed the opportunities that were given him to take an active role in international affairs. He was nominated as Australia's representative to the Commonwealth Group of Eminent Persons and played a role in ending apartheid in South Africa. This and other experiences on the international circuit advanced his thinking and led to change.

Malcolm Fraser is comfortable with that change. To the suggestion that Australians regarded him more warmly in later years than they did in the past he agreed.

And, yes, YOU can – begin again, be fearless, become something new, dare, say "next", keep the flame, and learn to change.

Being old The story about growing old is not the story of a body no longer able to perform up to your hopes or expectations. It is not the story of accumulated years. It is certainly not about a mind that is slow in functioning, aberrant and dislocated. No, it is the reality of thinking old, of living in our past and aimlessly drifting through the days as they come.

"I remember…" and "I remember when…" can become the signature tunes of a backward looking mind. There is nothing wrong with remembering. We should be able to recall all those we have known and valued in our lifetime. In one way or another many of them will have passed out of our lives. Over time they will be remembered increasingly vaguely, but they will remain as markers of shared experiences and new self-discovery.

Alex Barlow remembered Norm. Just Norm. He didn't have any other name for him. When they met their families were on a camping trip. He says "Maybe I was six or seven at the time. I have no image of 'Norm'. No real recollection of that camping holiday with my family. All I remember is a boy whose name remains with me because I first learned with his name the mnemonic device of rhyming a name with something familiar. "I'll remember your name," I said, "because Norm rhymes with 'form'."

A memory, but, not just a memory, rather a marker along life's way. That's what memory should be for. Remember the people known, the places experienced, the events that happened and the goals aimed for and achieved as markers, but not just as markers of a life lived and done. Rather use your memories to stimulate you to the enjoyment of people still to be known, as Cecile Dorward did as she travelled strange countries in her campervan. Use them to encourage you to travel to new places and experiences, as Dagmar Gilfelt did. Use them to look for new challenges and to make new beginnings as the poet Judith Wright did. Above all use them to set new goals.

As we grow older it is easy to become backward looking. Staying young as we age, however, calls for us to be forward looking. We only look back so as to be able to look forward. The memories we hold of people known, places seen, events experienced and of goals set and achieved should not just be markers of the past, of a life lived and done with. To an extent they are that, of course, but they should above all be sign posts pointing us on to new paths, to new experiences, to fresh places and to new beginnings.

Laurie Daley retired after twenty years as an outstanding Australian Rugby League footballer. In those years he represented his school, his town, his State and his country as a player and as his team's captain. Teams he played in won regional, national and international championships. He retired with a bag full of memories of players and games, enough to fill a book. In fact writing a book was the first thing he did after he retired. But in one's early thirties, at the end of a successful sporting career, no matter how financially well placed one may be, it is not the time to think old and start being old. For Daley, as for so many other successful sports persons, the end of a sporting career is the beginning of a new life and for journeys down new pathways, pathways that their sporting memories point to.

For Daley and people like him, memories are their launching pad. They are their signposts pointing to the direction their lives might now take.

Staying young means looking back only to see where the signposts are pointing and moving on down the paths that they are pointing to.

Moving on For young men like Laurie Daley moving on is the name of the game, at least so long as they see the chance to move on and have the will to do so.

For a lot of people, however, moving on may not be an option or not an option they want to choose. Many have spent long years working at the same job and at the best level that they can attain. Moving on in this instance could mean re-skilling, up-grading qualifications, changing employment, thinking self-employment and even radical self-assessment. These could be scary things for a person to contemplate. At the very least they call for a major shift from one's comfort zone. That's where the crunch comes. Moving out of one's comfort zone isn't the easiest of options.

Others have come to the end of their

working careers. Those careers may have spanned up to fifty long and arduous years of varying success. Now they are over. They may no longer want or have the need financially or socially to move on.

Retirement means freedom from the pressures of the work place, from the need to produce, to achieve, to be innovative, to compete and to contribute. It means, too, freedom to adopt a relaxed lifestyle freed from the rigid timetabling of a working life. Unfortunately, not everyone welcomes retirement, especially if it is forced on you through the process of redundancy. For many retirement is something that is accepted reluctantly, seeing in it the demolition of a structure that has held their life together, given them identity and direction, and provided a social context and a standard of lifestyle. For some it can be equivalent to a death sentence. Moving on may not be within their contemplation, and yet for them it is a real necessity. For them the question is not "Do I want to move on?", but it's "What do I move on to and how do I do it?"

Whether moving on means stepping out of one's comfort zone, making the choice to re-skill and to invent a new career or radically re-focusing one's life, it remains of the very essence of the process of staying young while growing old. At no stage in one's life should you shelve the option of moving on. Least of all should you do so because the turning of the page of a calendar, or the arbitrary decision of someone with some control over our lives, or social convention decrees that we are old, too old to do anything else of use.

Lewis Carroll's verses about Father William in *Alice's Adventures in Wonderland* classically sum up the pros and cons of the case. Father William has a son who expects him to act his age. He cannot understand why his father behaves in ways not suited for a man of his age. Father William finds his sons remarks very annoying. He tells his son to stop it otherwise he will throw him down the stairs.

Four things about Father William: he didn't believe that age had addled his brain; he still had an eye to making money; he had no problems saying what he wanted to say; he wasn't going to stand for anyone questioning his right to act in an unorthodox manner. No matter how often his son tried to force his advanced age on him, he had no time to waste listening to his negatives. Father William had no problems with staying young. His only problem was a well-meaning son determined to have his father 'be his age'.

Being your age What does the calendar tell you about yourself? No more than the number of years (months, days, hours, seconds) of life that you have experienced. It does not and it cannot tell you or anyone else how old or how young you are. We have all met men and women in their twenties, thirties and forties who are old, old, old! Set in their ways, backward lookers, small ambitions achieved and no more expectations – in the words of the poet Louis MacNeice's Bagpipe Music: "Sit on your arse for fifty years and hang your hat on a pension."

At the same time we have all known men and women whom we can properly call ageless. People in the autumn of their years but with the warmth of maturity in the vitality of their lives and the spring of youth in their forward-looking thinking, spry people.

No, being old or being young has nothing to do with age as such. Nor does it have to do with the symptoms of physical ageing. But it does have to do with the evidence of mental ageing. People do not grow old. They grow old when they stop growing.

By 'growing' we mean, of course, growing in the mind, and in the whole person, as well as the daily regrowth that occurs in the bodily process. People 'stop growing' when they let their minds age to the point where their minds no longer control the ageing of their bodies.

The emphasis is placed on the individual's choice in the matter of growing old.

Staying young regardless of age calls on the individual to make a deliberate choice of staying young and then to take the action that staying young calls for.

How do you answer the question, so often asked on birthdays, "How old are you?" Consider responding, "This year I am celebrating my twenty first birthday". "But you are not 21!" You could say, "No, but I was cut off by floods from attending my original twenty first birthday party, so this year that's the birthday I plan to celebrate. This year I'm really going to be 21 again!" Or maybe it will be your hundredth, just to make sure you celebrate it with a young mind. Or again it could be your fiftieth or fortieth since these are supposed to be rites of passage years for many people.

The real answer to the question, of course, is "I don't know". At any time in our life's journey we have three ages: our chronological age, our biological age and our psychological age. As was earlier pointed out, the calendar is no true indicator of real age. Two persons born at exactly the same time, on the same day and in the same year, on completing their fiftieth year may present the one like a thirty year old, the other like an eighty year old. The process of biological ageing varies not only from person to person, but within the bodies organs themselves. One person's hair turns grey in her late thirties, another's retains its natural colour into her late seventies or longer. But the grey-haired one at seventy may have the keenness of eyesight of a twenty year old, whilst the other's eyesight may have begun to fade in her late twenties.

No two bodies are alike at the same age.

At no age will any two persons have the same psychological age. To share the same psychological age people would have to have had exactly the same life experiences. Your psychological age will be the age you think yourself to be, the age you tell yourself that you really are and the age that overall you feel yourself to be. It will not be an age that you can express in years. It will not be an age that your body says you are. It will be the age that a total assessment of yourself, of your mind/body relationship, says that you are.

We don't have to stop playing because we are old; we grow old because we stop playing.
George Bernard Shaw

Anna Lundgren, at age 101, said, "Back in Norway where I was a little girl, when people got to be 55 or 65, they just sat. I never felt that old. That's old. I don't feel that old today", (cited in Deepak Chopra, 1993:68).

It is evident that staying young as our body ages biologically and chronologically will greatly depend on our remaining psychologically young. Being your age, then, is to be the psychological age you have set yourself to be.

Setting your age   But is it possible to remain psychologically young in a biologically and chronologically ageing body?   Can we really set our own psychological age?

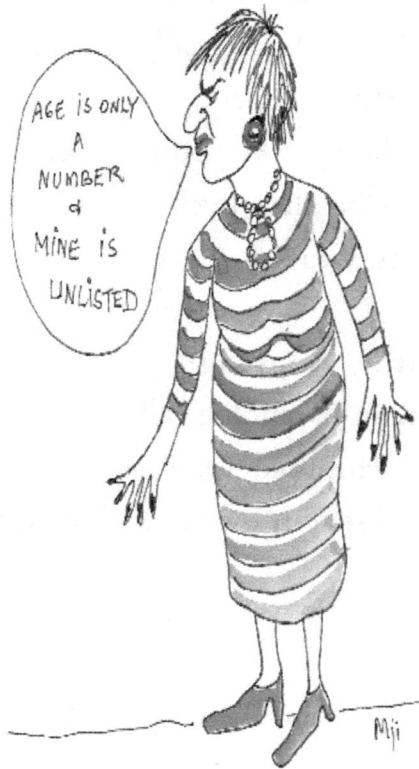

Yes we can. Other people all around us do all the time, so why not us? It's no great secret. All it takes to stay young is to think young. Setting your own psychological age means keeping a young mind, a mind that is as open now as it ever was to moving on, to learning, to new beginnings, to challenges, to new experiences, to meeting strangers and to forming new friendships.

Remember again how fearless you were when you were very young. Fearlessness is just one of the qualities of a young mind. We need to remind ourselves what those qualities are, and see how we can maintain them in ourselves so as to be able to echo in our own lives Archie the Cockroach's summing up of the ageing Mehitabel the Cat, "There's a dance or two in the old dame yet"…

3. COMING TO BE

Anyone who stops learning is old, whether at twenty or eighty. Anyone who keeps learning stays young. The greatest thing in life is to keep your mind young.

Henry Ford

Being one's self   Traditionally, Australia's Indigenous people have believed that their whole being is established from the moment that their spiritual identity is announced. This may happen shortly before or just after birth.   One or other parent may observe an unusual phenomenon – a perente lizard standing upright to block the parent's path, a species of fish leaping from the water close to the parent, a screeching parrot flying suddenly from a nearby bush.   This will tell the parent the totemic group that the child belongs to. That will be the child's personal totem throughout life and it will define a whole area of relationship and responsibility to the totemic group who share that totem, to the species of plant, bird, mammal, reptile, fish or insect that is his/her totem and to the spirit from which the totem originates.

Then, from their parents they inherit their family ancestry, which gives them rights and responsibilities in both their father's and their mother's family country. From the social organization of the group that their family belongs to, they are given their social position in relation to those who are not members of their immediate family. Among other things this tells them who, among these other families, are potential marriage partners. It also defines for them the sorts of relationship they may have with other people in their extended family and group connections – who can be their friends, who they can play with and later work with, and who they have to avoid.

Every Aboriginal person has a role to play in contributing to the well-being of his/her family and to the group to which his/her family belongs. Children must be taught the proper respect to be shown various members of their immediate family, and the forms of appropriate behaviour that are to be observed with each person in a relationship. For instance, four young girls in Arnhem Land in Northern Australia are playing together, but the youngest of them is called "Mother" by the other three and they treat her with the same respect as they would show to their own mother. Why? Because she is in fact their mothers' youngest sister, with a right to be called "Mother" by her sisters' children.

Children must also learn the forms of language which they will use in their relationship with other people. If their parents speak different languages or dialects of a language, the children must learn both.

As to their family's economics, each child, boy and girl, learns from its earliest days the strict principles of caring and sharing which define how the product of the days foraging and hunting are to be shared within the family group. A story from the Maung people on the North Goulburn Island, called Waira, tells how Ambidj the Rainbow Serpent swallowed up a whole village of people because a little boy there was making such a fuss about having an advance share of the yams and lily roots his grandmother was cooking for the family meal. Such stories were told to teach children the principles of caring and sharing.

The importance of the parents establishing the child's spirit source, its personal totem, is that it establishes from the very beginning of its life the child's essential being. It tells where the child's spirit has come from and where it will return to when it departs its body. It establishes the spiritual responsibilities the child will share throughout its life with those who share its totem. Most importantly it maps the path the child will follow as it grows to spiritual and social maturity. That path will take the child through a series of spiritual initiations which will begin at puberty and continue, so long as the person accepts the responsibilities that go with the knowledge that they will acquire, until in their middle or later years they have become masters of all the law that is theirs to learn. In these initiations what they are is revealed to them step by step. With each initiation the social and spiritual self which was theirs from the moment of their spiritual conception is unveiled. They learn progressively, as does the community to which they belong, who and what they are. Each initiation moves them to a higher grade of spiritual and social responsibility. From being minor performers in ceremonial ritual, they become ritual leaders and managers. Now, too, they become the elders, charged with watching over the law for their group, being the decision makers, the judges, the peace keepers, the negotiators, guardians of the group's traditions and knowledge and the teachers who see that the young men and women, over time, come to know who and what they are. But this passing through the fullness of the law to attain senior status among their people is not an inevitability. Seniority is the privilege of those who respect the law and accept the responsibilities each new revelation of law brings.

Being yourself, then, in the Australian Indigenous tradition means achieving the fullness of the identity that each person possesses from the moment of his/her spiritual conception.

For other Australians, as for many other peoples around the world, their self is not something they possess from the beginning that remains to be revealed. Rather their self is yet to become, and perhaps to become and become again.

Realising one's self   Sociological theory generally accepts that who we perceive ourselves to be, our 'persona', is the result of the many life experiences and influences, external and internal, which we have consciously or unconsciously allowed to shape us. According to this theory the whole of our life should involve us in the process of becoming something other than what we presently are. We are all born with the potential to become more than what we are at birth. At one level there is the potential for physical growth, more or less determined in our inherited genes. At another level there is the potential for our intellectual development which could well depend, at least in part, on the educational opportunities available to us. Social status, interpersonal relationships, economic role, personality, all of these are within our potential but may be shaped as much by others as by ourselves.

It is important for us to realise as early as possible in life that we are in this process of becoming something new, so that we can set ourselves to control and not be controlled in the process. We cannot, of course, control chaos, the source of the unexpected in our lives. Nor can we avoid the influences that parents, teachers, siblings and peers expect to and do impose on us in what are called 'the formative years' of our lives. Control comes from being aware that we are in a lifetime process of becoming and that what we may become lies ultimately within our choice. And that is true not only for the 'growing' years of our lives but for all the years. We all are in the process of coming to be from the very beginning up to the very end of our lives. It is a process we cannot stop, and should not want to stop. We know that we cannot stop the physical process of becoming. That was set in train at conception and will continue for the life of the body. But equally we cannot stop our potential to come to be something more intellectually, socially and personally, whether we want to or not.

A dear friend passed away not so long ago

after a full lifetime of coming to be something new. The critical stages when he made life changing decisions which led him down new life paths have been identified. He went through new learnings and new experiences, something other than he saw himself to be.

In his school days he was given a leadership role, captain of sports teams, prefect and so on. There was early recognition of his ability to accept responsibility and to perform at a high level. At university he performed creditably in his studies and excelled in sport. Called on to join a leading professional football team, playing at the top grade level, even though he played as an amateur, he found himself deprived of his status as a University sportsman. But for him the challenge of competing at the highest level of his chosen sport was more important than boasting of being a "University Blue".

War brought a major change to his life. Already enrolled in the University Regiment, there was no question but that he should join the Australian Air Force in whatever capacity he may be required. His studies were put aside and to war he went. He served with honour and valour and survived to be able to return to his studies.

He graduated with a Bachelor of Law degree and became a Barrister. He had a distinguished career in law despite becoming visually handicapped in his early fifties. He had an extraordinary memory for detail and for precedent cases in the law, and continued to practise before the highest courts in the country well into his seventies. He wrote many successful, humorous books to do with the law. Up until he died at 85 he was still fond of dredging up funny legal stories from the endless collection he had gathered over the years.

He left behind him a family of lawyers after two marriages. His was not, perhaps, the most remarkable life for a man of his background and for his era. But it well illustrates the process of 'coming to be in life'.

Rites of Passage All societies throughout time have used some form of ritual to mark the major socio-physical changes that take place normally in a person's life. Modern societies may not, perhaps, use the formal rituals that were common not so many years ago, but they still do use some form of ritual. Once, and for some people still, a child's social identity was marked with a naming rite, more often than not in some form of religious ceremony.

The result is not so considerably different to the identification of an Australian Indigenous child's totemic identity. Such a ceremony not only gives the child its family identity, but it also gives it a religious identity and establishes a range of extra-family relationships based on that identity. In some families god-parents are involved in a gift-giving relationship with their god-children which lasts throughout childhood. A continuing element of this naming and identifying rite is the formal recording of it with the registrar of births, marriages and deaths.

A major physical and social change in each person's life is that from childhood to adulthood. For most young people now the passage is marked not by any formal religious or public rite so much as by a change from one form of schooling to another. There are religious ceremonies, still commonly used, like Confirmation in the Christian Church and the Jewish Bar-Mitzvah. Intriguing is the way many Australian schools are now imitating the American tradition of a graduation ceremony for Year 6 Primary School children as they leave to begin their High School years. Yet it seems appropriate since this passage comes at a time when these young students are moving into puberty, and are making a major social change.

What are the rituals which mark the passage from youth to full adulthood? For young men it used to be the twenty first birthday celebration, being given the key of the door, being able to marry without first requiring parental consent and being given by the State the adult franchise carrying the right to vote.

For young women it was the debut, the formal admission into society and recognition that they were marriageable. Laws vary from place to place regulating the ages at which young people can be acknowledged as sufficiently adult to marry, to be licensed to drive, to leave home and obtain government support to do so, to enter into debt and to vote.

Socially marriage has been, and remains, one of the major rites of passage to change. It is always marked by ritual, even if that is no more than signing a declaration of freedom to marry, and filling out the marriage forms in the marriage registry. Some people now like to devise their own wedding rituals around the legal procedures, whether they are to be married in Church or by a marriage celebrant. There are those who, with or without ritual, choose to take on the responsibilities and privileges of married life but eschew marriage itself. Under modern law there is no impediment to their doing so. There are legal rituals, too, for those who seek to end their marriage through divorce, but there are few recognised religious or social rituals for doing so.

Apart from the many religious rites of passage, societies create their own such rituals to recognise success in achieving educational, artistic, intellectual, sporting, humanitarian, professional and other social goals which offer new social status and opportunity to the person achieving them. Note, for instance, the solemnity of the degree conferring ceremonies at most universities, and the passing out parades at military academies.

The only rite of passage for those growing old is the memorial service for the dead.

Enjoy life! There's plenty of time to be dead

Why should that be? Surely the passage from the summer to the autumn of one's life should be marked in ceremony with all the colour and change that marks the passage of the seasons in nature! After all if the rites of passage mark the important moments in our life when we are seen to be becoming socially and physically something more than we have been, surely the passage to seniority deserves its ritual, and not just the ritual of the retirement handshake or the presentation of a Seniors Card!

When Alex Barlow passed the chronological mark of 75 years some family and friends gathered for celebrations and speeches. He was very grateful, especially for the donations of good Scotch and Irish whiskies. Yet the occasion seemed less than significant to him.

He said he appreciated one of his birthday card messages which said "Take on the next twenty-five years, with energy and vigor and the production of many new enterprises".

Alex decided "Yes" that was certainly his intention. He planned his projects that he wanted to achieve and he set a timetable for their completion.

This book is the result one of those projects.

Why? Because he well knew that staying young in spirit, mind and action was important for him as time would take a toll on his body.

Like the senior Australian Indigenous men and women in their communities, Alex still had much to give. To stay young in the ways that he could was going to help him to go on giving.

If Alex could help other older people find ways to stay young too as they go on giving, then more and more people will find that growing old may carry much more pleasure for them than they imagined it ever could.

Becoming and becoming again   Regardless of whether or not there is a ritual recognition of one's moving on into one's senior years, for all of us the process of becoming, psychologically, physiologically, socially, emotionally and personally is inevitable.   We should not, indeed we cannot resist it.   But we can control it, we can use it and we can benefit from it.

We can control it by recognising its inevitability and preparing ourselves to be the new self we are in the process of becoming. That could mean, for instance, recognising the physiological changes that are taking place and making adjustments to our life style accordingly. We may need to adjust our diet, alter the forms of physical exercise we use, pay more attention to our health and so on.

My grandmother started walking five miles a day when she was sixty. She's 97 now, and we don't know where the heck she is.
Ellen DeGeneres

We can use the inevitability of becoming something new to review the direction our lives have taken and to explore the possibilities of change. One thing we can do is to assess the special knowledge and skills areas we have developed in the past with a view to enhancing them in the future, to applying them more effectively or to adding new knowledge and skills that seem appropriate for the person we are in the process of becoming.

Here is the sort of career change a lady made when she turned sixty. She had spent twenty years as a real estate agent during which time she had developed great knowledge about real estate and skill in helping people to define their real estate needs and then finding the property which met those needs. But at age sixty she found her work becoming routine and her approach to her clients less than enthusiastic. Time for a change, she thought, and she soon found another opportunity. She applied and got the job of raising awareness of the housing needs of the aging members of the community. For those entering their senior years there was a need for advice on their potential housing needs as they planned their coming years. For government and the building industry advice on the housing needs of the ageing was needed to ensure that there was an adequate supply of affordable town houses and units close to shops and transport. This lady did her job well and she felt her age and previous experience helped her to understand the older people she deals with.

There was one new skill that she added soon after taking up the job. She found a computer on her office desk, so she promptly signed up for after work lessons so that she could use this most modern specimen of office equipment.

And, yes, we can benefit from the inevitability of the ageing process of becoming new through change. Knowing that we cannot resist it, we should put our minds to planning how we can use the changes productively.

The future can be faced in two ways: either filled with apprehension or it can be filled with feelings of anticipation . It's anticipation if we decide to stay young. Jim Rohn (1994 :23) says people with apprehension worry all the time and neglect to plan their future. While they might plan to give up work and retire they don't plan how they are going to live their lives attitudinally.

One of the major effects of the process of

becoming is the social changes it can bring. Leaving one's work place and associates after many years inevitably brings a dramatic social change in one's life. There is a change of that status that one held on the job as well as of any relationship which may continue with one's former associates.

This sort of change is inevitable. To prepare for it we need to be able to open up our access to wider social contexts and hence to a wider range of friendships. To do this we need to identify our special interests. Call them 'hobbies' if you want.

One man remembers how he developed a collection of old post cards. It was based on some old cards that he had found at home in a sideboard drawer. They dated from the early 1900s and had simply been discarded in the drawer and forgotten. He wished that he still had them. Not because of their value, though they would have been valuable to a professional collector. Rather they, along with the many post cards that he collected on overseas trips, could give him entrée to associations of card collectors, to status among them and possibly to valued new friendships.

When Alex Barlow was visiting a friend in Basle, in Switzerland he learnt about the major annual festival in Basle called 'Fastnacht'. This aroused an interest in researching the forms of local festivals celebrated in Australia.

There is no end to the variety of interests that catch the attention of individual men and women. Sport, the arts, food, drink, cinema, - you name it and you will find that there are others who share the interest. Nor should we wait until the process of becoming has faced us with the reality of the new. Rather, knowing that we are moving into a new stage of our lives we should have already begun to prepare for it by choosing the new interests we intend to pursue, by setting out to develop them and by making such preparations as may be necessary to ensure that we can achieve the goals that we have set for them.

It is important that we accept that we are constantly faced in life with the process of becoming something other than what we are. In part we can accept the Australian Indigenous belief that at birth the potentiality of what we might be is already there, and that life is a process of revealing what and who we are.

Certainly we all are born with the potential to become whatever we choose to be. Certainly we can accept that we ourselves, and significant others who become part of our lives, can help to reveal who and what we may be. Equally certainly we are in a constant process of becoming something new, and how well we handle that process will depend on how well we control it, use it and plan to benefit from it.

4. YES, THERE IS TIME

Nobody grows old merely by living a number of years. We grow old by deserting our ideals. Years may wrinkle the skin, but to give up enthusiasm wrinkles the soul.
Samuel Ullman

For many of us accepting the inevitability of the process of becoming, the reality of constant change isn't easy. It isn't easy because we are comfortable with what and who we are. We have no wish to step outside our area of comfort. Whatever change is forced upon us we will adjust to. We will do so unwillingly, reluctantly, and, so far as we can, we will try to maintain the life that we have become accustomed to. Besides we feel it's too late for us to start to become something new.

But, really, is it ever too late?

An eighty-six year old man led a group of

retirees on a nearly 900 kilometre bike ride from Melbourne to Sydney. The group of riders wanted to show that age was no barrier to doing exciting things.

My mother, Doreen, at the age of 71 years graduated from university with a Bachelor of Arts Degree in professional writing. She went on to publish a book of religious verse and had to do a reprint after her first print run sold out.

There are so many people who are not afraid to step out along a new path regardless of their age. Those who are afraid do not so much fear the new as they fear time. "I'm 70 – 80 – 90", they'll say. "If I started something new now I might not have the time to finish it".

So what? Finishing isn't so important. Starting is.

Remember Parkinson 's Law? "Work expands so as to fill the time available for its completion". His concept was that if you could do the job in 5 days but you are given 10 days to do it, then you will drag out the work to make it last for the 10 days. The difference for the older person is that there is no time to waste. There is time, but it is not there to fritter away. The work to be done is to be done in the minimum of time available for it. In other words for the older person time management is even more important than it may be for business people. As the saying goes, for business people 'Time means money'. For the older person time means much more as there is inevitably less of it.

The importance of starting An American teacher spends a lot of her time encouraging and teaching people to write their life story. But she does not see publishing these stories as the main point of the exercise. Telling the story is what is most important for each person. We each have a story. It may not seem an impressive nor exciting story, but it is our story. It is true that to take a person's story away from them could destroy that person. Sadly we see people who no longer have any memory of their life story, no knowledge any more of who they are and what they have been. Without their story they have become nothing people, with no connection to their surroundings and little or no relationship with the loving ones who continue to care for them. So, for each of us, telling our story in writing can be the way to make sure that we keep our story and value it. If that is what we want to do, then getting started is what will matter most.

Whatever new path we decide to explore, once we have identified where we want to go, what we want to do, then getting started is the most important step to take.

An audience was asked what a marathon runner had to do to run a marathon. Some said train. Some said get into condition. These are things to do, perhaps, to prepare to run a marathon. But to actually run the marathon the runner has to start. Take that first step, run that first 100 metres, pass the first kilometre mark, run and run and run, focused on the next marker and the next and the next, until the race is run. None of us can go anywhere until we start.

Start what? The choice of what you start is up to you. Maybe you have a new business venture in mind. Maybe there is something you want to make. Maybe there is a project group you want to join, like a fitness group, a Tai Chi class, a life drawing or other art group. There has to be something that could interest you and challenge you. It doesn't have to be something entirely new. It could be a challenge to take what you have been doing a further step.

There is a fountain of youth: it is your mind, your talents, the creativity you bring to your life and the lives of people you love. When you learn to tap this source, you will truly have defeated age.

Sophia Loren

Once you know what it is that you want to do, do it. And don't let anyone dissuade you. There will be any number of people who think that they know what is best for you, and what you want to do isn't one of them.

There was a man who wanted to construct a boat. He started reading yachting and boat designing magazines. His family indulged him up to the point where he had decided on the boat that he wanted to make. But when he started to source and price the materials he would need, and started to prepare his under-house workshop area the family suddenly realised that he was serious! No longer indulgent, the family made his project THE FAMILY JOKE. They shared it with visitors. Laughed at it with his friends. Refused to take his project seriously. Told him he'd never get it done. Boat building is no longer on his agenda.

Preparing to start If one were planning to run a marathon, common sense would dictate sensible preparation, like making sure one was fit enough to run the distance, had the right sort of running gear, had the assistance of a qualified trainer, made a study of the course to be run and had officially entered for the run. Preparing to run isn't running the race, but it is a necessary part of it. Obviously one should not attempt to run a marathon until one's preparation is successfully completed.

Sometimes your preparation might be very simple. To find out about Tai Chi or yoga classes, for instance, all you might need to do is to do a Google search to get details for your area.   Maybe you will need to check with your doctor in case there is any medical reason why you should not do this form of exercise.   The cost of the classes might also be significant for you.   All being well, that's all the preparation you may need.   Enroll, turn up to classes and soon you will be well on your way with your exercise program.

On the other hand, sometimes your preparation may be complex and extended. Your project will really start with your preparation.   Suppose you have had a lifelong ambition to be an actor.   Study, work, family have all prevented you in the past, but you have rightly decided that it is never too late to start.   A local repertory company is auditioning for a new play.   You turn up at the audition offering to read for one of the minor roles.   You are accepted and instructed to turn up next day for the first reading of the play.   Your acting career has begun, but you have much work to do before the play's first night! Among other things you may have to learn to act. Yours may only be a minor role, but many a play's success has depended as much on the performance of the actors in the minor roles as on the performance of the actors in the leading roles. You will not want to let the rest of the cast down by a poor performance, so you will do what you can to develop your acting skills.

New learning is often part of preparing to start something new. Taking acting lessons, for instance, if one had decided to become an actor. One man decided that on retirement he would do a course in landscape design. He was moving to a small rural property and wanted to be able to work on developing an attractive landscape on that property. He also had it in mind that he might find some work locally in this field.

First, though, came the new learning. Incidentally, new learning doesn't always require enrolling in some formal course or other.   More often than not we can find all the information and instruction that we may require in a do-it-yourself manual, a how-to book or on the internet.   Of course being open to new learning is one of the most important requirements for staying young as we grow old.   After all, most of us spend all of our working life time learning.   We may have to learn to use new technology and become proficient in using the computer. We have to keep up-to-date with developments in our profession or trade.   We have to adjust to new working arrangements and conditions.

As ophthalmologists moved into laser eye treatment they had to install proper equipment and learn how to work it.   They had also to learn what conditions could be relieved by the treatment, and in each instance had to evaluate its likely effect on a particular patient.   Staff had to travel overseas to get clinical experience with the new equipment.

They continue to learn as new forms of laser technology came onto the market.

Ours is a society that constantly calls on all of us to learn to operate new social systems as well as new technology. The principles of 'downsizing' require that those remaining in a 'downsized' workplace become multi-skilled so as to do the tasks that will now fall to them. The principles of 'outsourcing' require that those made redundant in their workplace by having their work outsourced now move to doing a different kind of work, or else put themselves into the marketplace to compete to provide to their former employers the same services that they were formerly employed to do. Whether one is 'downsized' or 'outsourced' there is new learning to be done. Whether in the workplace or not there is always new learning to be done.

Some time back we had our home of fifteen years demolished to make way for a new development on the site. Until our new home was completed we lived in rented accommodation. Our previous home was quite large and allowed for office space for three people, with a research library of around 3000 books and hundreds of journal articles and professional journals. In our temporary accommodation there was no room for this library nor for at least half of the furniture which the former house contained. The furniture, the library shelving and much of the office equipment we were able to sell or give away. What remained, including the boxes of papers and books, overflowed in the temporary accommodation? We had to learn how to maneuver around boxes stacked in the bedrooms and other private areas, as well as accustoming ourselves to the technology of the temporary home.

Some months later we had to do it all again when we moved back to the brand new home! We were only about a kilometer from our previous home, but we still needed to remind ourselves not to make the familiar turns that took us there in the past. We had to learn the best bus for us to travel on and the nearest bus stop. One important new learning was the need to plan the shopping and to make a list of the things we need as they run out. Previously the nearest shops were only a short walk away across the road. Now we needed to drive to the shops if we were caught short of the staples - milk, bread, butter, sugar and so on. Does it annoy you when you need to slice an onion into the dish you are preparing, and find that you have run out?

Preparing to start is actually the beginning for many enterprises – you start buying in the timber for the shed you plan to build, you have enrolled in the art class that is going to get you started as an artist. However, there may still be a few stumbling blocks between preparing to start and actually getting under way.

Neither the first nor the last A university lecturer used to constantly exhort his students not to be the first to take up new theories, nor to be the last to accept them once they had been established.   That is a sound principle to work on, especially now when people are being exposed through the media in its myriad forms to inventions and discoveries, and to new ideas almost as soon as they are formed.   There is no more need now to rush into the new than there ever was in the past. However, there is much more pressure now to do so than there ever was before. We can easily find ourselves adopting new technology that is as yet unproven, being persuaded to join some organization with an attractive slogan but no really substantial advantage to offer, or purchasing new placebos whose value rests on unscientific claims.

Unfortunately the decision as to whether or not to go along with the new doesn't always lie in our hands.   Take banking for instance. In the past a child could open their first bank savings account and be given a tin box to feed coins into. Each week the child could take a coin to school and the teacher would write the amount down on his tally sheet for the bank and make a note in the savings book. Each year, too, the bank would add a little interest as the savings grew.

Banks eventually moved away from the old bank savings passbooks. They moved into the era of internet banking and having people take their plastic card to an ATM or by using EFTPOS getting money from the supermarket.

Whether we like it or not, there are many changes in business conventions, technologies and attitudes that require us to accept the changes and learn how to live with them.

Of course, change in itself is not a bad thing. Sometimes, though, it is hard to see who is benefiting from a particular change. Mostly we prefer to be given time to consider whether or not we need to or want to make a particular change. If it is one that circumstances force us to make, like having a carbon tax, we at least expect to be told why we have to make the change and be allowed to argue about it. Better still if we can have a vote about it, before the government makes a decision for us.

Like forever advancements in technology, sooner or later the old systems that they are due to replace are faded out and we are forced to accept the new.

Change is in itself not a bad thing. The process of staying young while growing old calls on our being keen to look for and to experience the new. If long experience should make us cautious about change, and lead us to question who it is who actually benefits from the change, that should not prevent us from entering into the excitement of purposeful and useful change. After all most of us have lived through a lifetime of accelerating and extraordinary change.

Now we have instant communication like email and social media with any person or group of people anywhere in the world. A few hours by plane takes us to all parts of the world we want to visit. An international phone and video hook-up, and things such as Skype, can bring together leading professionals, business persons or politicians from all over the world in conference. In little more than a half a century we have seen mankind move from flying a plane barely above the ground to journeying into distant space, setting up human habitations on stations in space and even visiting the moon.

Every new year the media around the world carries reports setting out the 'achievements' and major events of the previous year. An interesting exercise you could do would be to make a list of what you think were the important achievements during your lifetime. Better still, gather a few friends around you and compare what you each think were the ten most important.

Accelerating change will always mark our future. Leading the way may well be the results of continuing research in the field of nanotechnology. There will be extraordinary advances in medicine based on our increasing knowledge of DNA and our exploration of the information contained in the Genome Project. These are just two of the exciting changes that lie ahead. We do live in the age of the new.

The challenge for each of us in staying young is to be excited by and interested in these changes and, where there is the opportunity, to embrace them. We may not always fully understand the nature or the workings of these changes. That doesn't matter. You may know the principle of the internal combustion engine, but you may not have the faintest idea of what to do with the engine of your car should anything go wrong.

However, that doesn't stop you enjoying driving the latest model computerised, press button car.

To stay young keep up to date as well as you can with changes in your trade, in your profession, in whatever was your working field of expertise. Have you looked at a residential building site recently? Take a look at the range of new materials builders have to choose from and the new types of tools that the workmen work with. Anyone who has worked as an architect, a master-builder or a building tradesman/woman most of their lives or in any other specialised field, would need to maintain their interest by keeping up to date with the latest innovations and developments and, most importantly being able to talk to others who remain active in their field. This is keeping the mind young, alert and interested.

A young mind is important for staying young.

Now I Begin   Are you the kind of person who, after all the planning and preparation, still finds it difficult to actually start?   If you are then you are not alone.

Alex Barlow had this great idea of setting up a data-base of Australian festivals. He sent questionnaires out to all local government authorities.   He collected festival brochures from all over Australia.   He filed the information and categorised the various festivals by type, by season, and so on. A calendar of events was drawn up and he visited and spoke with organisations involved in the tourist industry to establish the viability of such a data-base.   The whole history of festivals in Australia was researched and analysed the information that had been assembled was incorporated into conference papers. Alex wrote an article on Festivals for a prestigious book on Australian folklore. He did all of this but failed to set up his data base. What beat him was technology. It was an era when internet technology had not quite made the advances it now has. What was difficult for him in the past would have been much easier today.

Eventually, he threw away all the information that he had collected because the data was no longer current and had no more than remote historical value.

Alex learnt from this experience. He felt he should have limited his objective to the attainable, taking into account all the circumstances. He was comfortable in his planning and preparation, because gathering, collating and analysing data were within his area of expertise. To get his data-base operating, though, called for expertise that he did not possess, and was unable, at that time, to acquire. Nor could he afford to purchase it, even if he had known how to find someone who could do it for him.

In brief, then, if you have difficulty in getting started check to see whether or not it is because you have set yourself a task beyond your present ability.

Alex should have done this right at the start of his festivals project. The task that he had set himself was to establish a computerised data-base of current Australian festivals. His primary focus should have been on what he needed to do to set up a data-base on computer – find out what soft-ware program he would have needed and then learned how to use it. Or, alternatively, he could have outsourced the project and what it might have cost. Alex did neither so when it came time to start he was stopped in his tracks.

But suppose Alex had done all that he needed to do to set his task under way yet he could not bring himself to start. That could be only because he was afraid to start – afraid to make the final commitment, afraid of not having time to complete what he had set himself to do, afraid he might not succeed in doing it, afraid of what people may say and afraid of the demands it may make of him.

Stepping outside our 'comfort zone' is never easy. Nor is running a marathon. It takes that first step. But once you take it, it isn't so hard to take the next and the next. After all it is true, isn't it, that it is better to have run and lost than never to have run at all.

5. NEW FRIENDS

Life isn't about finding yourself. Life is about creating yourself.
George Bernard Shaw

It is inevitable that time is going to run out for the many people you have had the good fortune to work with and befriend during your lifetime. When you hear of this one or that one for whom there is no more time you wish that they have been able to keep their lives full and active, and that they have been content in their passing.

Rather than mourning your friends rejoice in their lives and respect the things they have achieved. At the same time rejoice in the new friends you have made, continue to make and seek to make.

For a number of reasons, death being only one of them, older people often seem to lose contact with their friends. Some leave town

or move across town.   Some go off to live
with their children.   Some move into a
retirement villages or age care facilities.   Some
just don't seem to come round any more.
Whatever the reason, one of the realities for
many older peoples is that their circle of
friendships seems constantly to narrow.

This chapter is about keeping friendships
alive and the importance of making new
friends. Why?   Because staying socially active
keeps us aware of what is happening to people
around us. It forces us to think beyond our
own little world and challenges us to take an
interest in the lives and concerns of other

people. It helps us to put our own lives and concerns in perspective.

With advancing years having friends is vital for your own mental health and well being helping you live a richer, fuller, happier and more fulfilling life. People who keep themselves alive and interested in life have no problems acquiring friends. Good friends become confidants, they encourage you, they are there for you when you are down and they provide intellectual stimulation and companionship.

Dale Carnegie (1989) wrote an entire book on how to make friends. He wrote it in 1937 and gave it the title *How to Win Friends and Influence People.* Here are some of his major points:

Be interested in others
Give honest and sincere appreciation
Praise people
Learn the other person's view
Understand things from their perspective

Show respect for other people's opinions

Smile

Remember a person's name

Be a good listener

Make the other person feel important

Everyone needs to be reminded of these key elements and keeping our friendships alive and making new friends will call for some effort on our part. Here are some ideas.

Keeping friends   Good friendships, like loving partnerships, have to be worked at. It is not up to your friends to maintain friendly contact, it's up to you. The type of friendship that we have with each of our friends will vary. With some we play golf, do yoga, meet for morning coffee, share a hand of bridge and generally do things together from time-to-time.

With others we may have a more intimate relationship. We play jokes on each other, laugh together, gossip, confide our deepest secrets, sympathise, explore ideas, reminisce, and generally enjoy each other's company whenever there is an opportunity to do so.

Other friendships are more formal. It may have grown out of a working relationship, out of a shared life changing experience like wartime service, from a professional relationship or some other reasonably long-term interaction.

The type of friendship that we share will determine the action we need to take to keep that friendship alive and meaningful. Have you ever attended a school reunion? Many have said that after years and years of no connection with old classmates that when they met again at a reunion it was a strange experience. Sometimes if you have all taken different paths in life it is not easy to re-establish that friendship of the past because you have nothing in common. You feel as if you are on a different planet. Perhaps with a few exceptions, these friendships may be too long neglected to be now resurrected.

No matter what the type of friendship, if you want to keep it work at it. Here are a few things you might do. Make a list of all the people you have been and still are friends with. Have you a collection of old address books? Ring them or write to their old address. Check them out in the phonebook. Ask around among people who might still have contact with them. You may find there names of friends whom you haven't seen for years.

A really excellent way of making connections with people that you know now and also of the past is to set up a Facebook account or check out other types of social networking on the internet. Stories tell of how people reconnect after many years even when they live in other parts of the world.

Some people are afraid to renew old friendships, not knowing what time may have done to their friends' lives or whether their former friendship would still be remembered and valued. Be that as it may, it will do no harm at any rate to go through the exercise of making a lifetime list of 'friends'. It will certainly be a mental challenge for you.

Being able to revive past friendships is one thing. More important is keeping alive our present ones. Again, make a list of all those you currently class as friends. Note alongside each name when and where you last saw each other. Is it your turn to invite them around? Should you pick up the phone, write, put a message on Facebook send a card, or write an e-mail? If necessary find a reason for you to get together, create an event, discover an anniversary, find a story to tell or something to show. Or simply suggest that you meet for coffee.

If you are assiduous in maintaining contact with friends well and good, but if you have begun to slacken off with your friendships, it might be time to go through the listing exercise that has been suggested. You might also need to think about why you have begun to let some friendships slip. Is it because you have to travel some distance, perhaps on public transport, to friends who do not live close by? Maybe it is because your life has taken a different direction or you have moved away to a new town to live.

Making contact may be difficult if you are no longer able to drive or have no one to call on to drive you. A sensible compromise might be to arrange to meet halfway. Daytime meetings might have to be the compromise for those who are reluctant to venture out at night. If, for good reasons, you are no longer able to venture far from home, then use your home as your function centre – morning teas, lunches, happy hours, dinner, barbeques, parties. You don't have to overdo it, of course. How frequently you entertain or set up meetings with friends is up to you. Some you may only need to meet once or twice a year. Others you may want to see or talk to several times a week. Once more frequency will depend on the nature of your friendship.

Always keep in mind the old caveat about not outstaying your welcome. You can overdo contact, no matter how close your friendship may be. Friends need their private space as much as you do. Give them room to get on with things important to them. It is very easy, if you'll pardon the language, to become a 'boring old fart'. You may find your latest medical experience an item of immense interest. Others almost certainly will not. If you must give a response to a genuine inquiry about your health do so succinctly, simply and positively.

Do you know anyone who can speak for an hour or more on their latest medical condition, linking it to past medical experiences of their own, of unknown friends of hers, of her family both present, past and present? Any reference to health, theirs or anyone else's, will set them off. Indeed, any topic of conversation, no matter what, will soon be directed back to health 'problems'. This sort of person is the epitome of a 'boring old fart'.

People who repeat the same stories, tell the same jokes, mount the same soapbox regardless of the occasion or the make-up of the audience of friends fall into the same category. They do so mainly because they make no effort to stay in contact with events in the changing world about them. Nor are they aware of or interested in the conversations going on around them. As soon as they can seize the floor, regardless of the flow of the previous conversation they will be off and away with their version of 'the world according to me'.

Have your friends begun avoiding you lately? Maybe it is time to start listening to yourself.

Exhaustipated
and
too tired to
give a shit!

Keep up to date at least in those areas that are likely to be of common interest to your friends. You don't have to be expert on everything. Never be embarrassed to admit your ignorance of a particular matter. Ask if you don't understand.

Alex Barlow tells a story of how he stood in for a friend, who was lecturing in a course in business communications. Part of the lecture was about setting up an Information Technology presentation. Among other items needed for the presentation was the Powerpoint. Of course, he thought, remembering back to his many classroom presentations, always check where the power point is. But no, as the students quickly informed him, the PowerPoint in this case was special software which enabled the lecturer to do a slide presentation. Alex said he made no claim to being any sort of an Information Technology buff, so he was not embarrassed at having the students correcting him. The continuing development of Information Technology, and its growing importance in so many aspects of our daily lives and in business, places on all of us a need to familiarise ourselves with these developments and their social and economic implications.

Some other areas that we might also need to keep up to date with are local, state, national and international affairs. Maybe you have read in your daily papers, or have seen on the television news, or consulted your iPad the debate on the refugee policy in Australia. Do you know about all the issues surrounding refugees or climate change. Do you have a view on these issues? It doesn't hurt to be passionate about something you have strong views on and have sound factual arguments to back up your stance. Sometimes though, for the sake of friendship, we may need to restrain our passions. Have you an interest in contemporary literature, poetry, music, theatre, film and the other visual and performance arts? All of these get considerable coverage in the daily and weekend press. At least you can make use of their reviews to find out which are the most interesting and best.

And then, of course, there is always sport!

The point is that keeping friendships fresh and fulfilling calls for effort on our part. We make the contact. We plan the event. We run our own friendship book and keep it up to date. We make the effort to stay in touch with the interesting things happening about us, aiming to be good listeners, alert guests and amusing hosts.

Making friends When you meet new people a good idea is to offer a business card to new people that you meet? And do you carry some blank cards for other people to put their details if they don't carry a business card. Become a collector of business cards. Record the people you meet into your friendship book.

Networking is a good skill to have. While networking may usually be associated with business become a networker to widen your friendship base. Depending on your interest areas you may go to art openings, book launches, business presentations, special luncheons, sporting events, attend environmental groups or join in the creation of a community garden.

All you need is a simple card with your name, address, phone and email address. When you meet someone whom you find interesting and whom you would like to know better, at a proper moment in the conversation present your card. You could say something like, "This is me and this is how to contact me. I find you an interesting person and I would enjoy hearing more about you and the things that you do. May I ring you sometime when I am planning to entertain friends and invite you to join us?"

What people are looking for is an exchange of cards as a step towards building up their file of contacts. The committed networker will have an extensive card file organised so as to give him/her access to different categories of people – occupation, interests, business and so on. Most likely they will maintain a computer file and will be able to call up a list of people who fit into a particular category. All of this of course has been taken a step further with Facebook and other social networking sites.

The value of keeping a list of people you meet and knowing a little bit about them means you might want to be able to check who is having a birthday today, or is celebrating some other significant anniversary. You might also want to be able to find the names of particular people to share an event with you. Suppose, for instance, that you have an opportunity to attend a local jazz festival and you are looking for a small group of friends to go with you. It would certainly help, wouldn't it, if you had noted on your cards those people who were jazz fans.

The point of all this is not to turn you into a collector of other people's cards. It is to show you one way to meet new people and, possibly, to widen your circle of friends. It will be up to you to decide how you will use your new card collection. Not everyone that you meet and exchange cards with will fall into the category of 'friend'. Nevertheless, it is still worthwhile keeping the cards on file in case you have need yourself, or someone that you know has a need for the kind of services that they may be able to supply.

In this day and age, when you ring a business firm or a government department, it is always easier to get service if you have a name and if you have a direct line to that person. Perhaps one of the more annoying innovations in communication technology has been the introduction of the answering by numbers system of getting to your information source. You know the sort of system that says when the number answers, "If you have an inquiry press one", "If you want to speak to an agent press two", "If you have a complaint press three", etc.

Alex has a story about trying to contact his bank. He said " I tried ringing a bank recently to query a charge on my credit card. A voice answered that if I had an inquiry I should press one. It then proceeded to inform me what I could get on two, three and so on. It also told me that as soon as I knew which number I needed to press I could press it without waiting to hear what I could get on the other numbers. After some thought I decided that I was making an inquiry, so I pressed one. This time the voice told me to enter the number of the bank that I had my account with followed by my account number and then press hash. I never can figure out which of the numbers on my account statement or cheque book represent the bank number, so I ignored that one and simply entered my credit card number believing that that was the appropriate number. It was, and I didn't really need the bank number since a voice came through with the usual, "Please hold, all our operators are busy {WHAT! BOTH OF THEM?}and we will get back to you soon". After their music presentation there was the operator in person ready to give me the third degree to ensure that I really was the owner of the account that I had named. With that out of the way, having heard my inquiry she was able to tell me that she couldn't help me in any way and that I would have to go to the nearest branch of their bank in person with my account to sort it out. I had thought to do that originally, but my account stated that if I had an inquiry I should ring the 1800 number listed on the account, so I did, and then off I went in person to the bank!"

The point of the story is that it is easier to get the information you need these days if you have a name and a direct phone number of someone rather than having to work through the press this, press the other system.

Volunteers and street parties The Australian armed forces in the First and Second World Wars were mainly dependent on volunteers. Most charitable organizations depend on volunteers. The bush fire brigades in every State and Territory in Australia are staffed by volunteers who continue to do a remarkable job laying their lives on the line to protect the lives and homes of their fellow Australians.

No doubt many of you have been volunteers at some time and may still be. One older friend records readings each week to be broadcast to people with reading difficulties. To do so she drives from her home in the country to the city an hour's drive away. Another friend works for Lifeline collecting and sorting books for its annual book sale.

In your home town or city you can find many opportunities to volunteer your services to help other people. In doing so you also open the opportunity to extend your circle of friendly contacts and so to make new friends. You don't have to travel far either to find a group of volunteers that you can join. They may be a church group, a group helping your local school, a neighbourhood sports group or a care group. Look around you. You may even have an idea for forming a group yourself where you have seen a need for providing a new voluntary service for your neighbours. The best thing about these local groups is that they meet locally, often in someone's home. You could host meetings of a volunteer group in your home. Joining a local group of volunteers can increase your interest in your own neighbourhood and help you to get to know better the people that you share it with.

How well do you know your neighbours and the people in your street?

Have you been to a street party lately, or joined in some local event – the annual school fete, for instance? At Christmas time our local Salvation Army Brigade holds a carols in the park evening. Families bring their rugs and picnic tea baskets and get into the spirit of the evening. The band plays in front of an aged care facility so that they too can sit and join in. The evening is always well advertised and provides an opportunity to invite neighbours and friends to join together for a happy evening. It is a popular local event and brings people together in friendship and sharing. Another popular local event is the annual fete at the aged care facility. Goods and goodies are donated. Volunteers, including a number of people from the facility itself, staff the stalls which line one side of the local shopping centre. Visitors and shoppers parade past the stalls making their selections, and greeting and chatting with the fete's volunteers. Such events are important since they help to freshen and renew both new and old friendships. They keep us young and in touch.

Friends, young and old   Your friends list should hold the names of people from all age groups.   It is very important that you do not restrict your friendships only to those people around your own age.   By sharing the interests, the concerns, the amusements and the explorations of friends from all age groups and across ethnic and other social groups it becomes possible for us to enter into the total reality of a world with which it is easy for us to lose touch as we grow old.   Doing so is another part of staying young.

Probably the best way to broaden the range of our friendships is to create events and functions which will have appeal to people of differing ages and social backgrounds.   They don't have to be major events and functions. You don't have to think in terms of lots of people and hours of pre-planning and preparation.

Work on the idea of meeting younger people.   Meeting with and making friends with people younger than yourself does not require that you pretend to be one of them, or that you attempt to join in their social activities. Staying young around younger people does not require us to adopt the fashions of the young, their entertainments or their 'in' language. What it requires is that we show them respect for their ideas, enthusiasm for their potential, a willingness to listen to and to try to understand their formulation of their world, admiration for their attempts – be they artistic, creative, sporting or whatever, and a readiness to consider seriously what they contribute to discussion.

As the years pass the nature of many friendships change. The young pursue their careers, they marry, they take on the parenting role, and their interests, their enthusiasms and their passions mature and may become more fixed. You may need to adapt to this change and accept that they may want to place their friendship with you on a different level. That's O.K! Both the making of friendships and being friends is a two way process.

For any number of reasons friendships lapse. No one is to blame. It just happens that way. For your part the important thing is to maintain your interest in the lives and activities of your friends, without in any way intruding on them. This may mean an occasional phone call "Just to see how everything's going". Or it could be a note on a post card, or nowadays an email or a message on Facebook. Just something, not too often, to let friends know that you still value them. If they respond, well and good. If not don't worry. There could be any number of reasons why people are unable to reply to our messages.

So working at making and keeping friends is one of the more important ways of staying young as the years roll on. Remember that it's up to you. Don't just sit there complaining that no one comes to see you anymore. You have to make the effort.

Making friends, having friends and seeing friends helps you to keep your life interesting, active, challenging – keeps you young. Have many friends, all kinds of friends, friends that you stay in touch with on a regular basis, and stay young.

6. HUGS AND KISSES

When did you last hug a friend?

Hugging makes you feel good. It provides comfort, helps combat loneliness and contributes to building self-esteem. There is a miniature book called *The Tiny Book of Hugs* which lists the benefits of hugging (Keating, 1992:10-11) It is even reputed to slow down ageing with huggers staying younger longer.

According to the Concise Oxford Dictionary the word came into the English language in the sixteenth century from the Scandinavian word "Hugga" meaning to console, to give comfort. A friend from the Australian town of Wagga Wagga is nicknamed "The Huggiest Hugga from Wagga Wagga". He is strongly into bear hugs which, in his case, can be a danger to ribs and breath.

There are many kinds of hugs that you can use, depending on who you are hugging and what you want to say with your hug. Where appropriate your hug may be accompanied by a kiss to cheek or lips. You can hug both men and women, though with discretion. Some men may see the hugging of another man as a 'bit effeminate'. And what is acceptable in one culture may not be acceptable in another.

Hugging someone when you first meet a person is not something you do on first acquaintance. If you are not in the habit of hugging anyone other than your spouse, your partner or your younger children, you should ease into hugging your close friends and companions carefully. If your companions in company greet each other with hugs it should be appropriate for you to do so too.

Members of sports teams often form a communal hug either before or after a game. This is acceptable in a number of sports, though you may be looked at askance if you offer to hug an individual sportsman or woman sometime before or after, or even during the game – with the exception, of course, of hugging the goal scorer, a common practice in soccer.

You may hug by way of greeting; you may hug to express affection; you may hug in sympathy; you may hug to declare support for your fellows; you may hug as part of a religious ceremony.

Gubboo Ted Thomas, an Australian Indigenous elder from New South Wales held a ceremony that he called he called a 'Humming Bee'. Several of the men and women would strip off their upper garments and then form with the others present a hugging circle. Gubboo stood in the centre of the circle and intoned a humming sound which the others in the circle took up. As its volume increased and the pitch rose the huggers clutched each other more closely and tightened the circle and swayed in rhythm. The effect of the humming was hypnotic and the huggers began to experience an intense spiritual, even mystical response. The 'Humming Bee' lasted for about 30 minutes. As it continued, one here and another there broke from the circle, and were somewhat dazed from the experience. Gubboo explained that his 'Humming Bee' was not entirely a traditional ceremony of the Yuin people. Rather it was a pulling together of the ceremonies of many indigenous religions and other religions that he had witnessed. Its purpose was to release the spiritual forces that lie in all of us, and to combine those forces through the 'Humming Bee' ceremony so as to help the huggers to share the spiritual forces that were so released.

There is much you can say to a person with a hug and, perhaps, even more that you can say about yourself. The important thing is not to be afraid to hug when you have the opportunity to do so.

Flirting   The hug used subtly may also form part of the art of flirting.   Do you remember the art of flirting?   It was something you probably did a lot of when you were young, before you settled on some special person.

Flirting is not to be confused with seducing!   Flirting is a game with clear rules and an agreed purpose.   Its purpose is to declare that one finds the person being flirted with amusing, attractive, stimulating, intellectually challenging and someone that you might like to have a close friendship with. The rules depend on the status of the partners to the flirtation.   If both are free of any binding relationship to a life partner the rules differ from those where such a relationship may exist for one or both persons.   The first rule in flirting is to keep your flirtation light and frivolous.   Once your interaction begins to become intense and intimate it ceases to be flirtatious.

As   much   as   possible   confine   your

flirtation to public places and to gatherings of people. As the saying goes, there is safety in numbers. Generally you will be flirting with a person of the opposite sex, though sexual attraction as such will not be the sole motivation for the flirtation. Joking will be an important part of it, as will be exaggerated compliments and declarations of attraction and affection. The presentation of small gifts, chosen for amusement more than to impress, is acceptable. Dining together in public is permissible so long as the conversation remains light and humorous, or at least not too serious. It is best not to attempt flirtation in private situations. Such flirting may be misinterpreted as an attempt at seduction.

A flirtation may be continued over a long period of time. It should be part of every couple's continuing relationship. You don't have to confine your flirting to outsiders. At the same time you don't have to confine your flirting to your continuing relationship. You would be wise, however, to speak openly and freely to your partner about your flirtatious activity.

Given that the purpose of flirting is to make another person feel good about themselves, and to express certain pleasurable responses that they stir in us, there is obviously no reason for restricting flirtations to the young. One is never too old to flirt. Flirting is really another way to tell a person that he or she is valued and appreciated, and the older we get the greater our need to be told. Indeed being told flirtatiously is part of the process of staying young.

Sex

...the intense yearning which each of them has for the other does not appear to be the desire of lovers' intercourse, but of something else which the soul of either evidently desires and cannot tell, and of which she has only a dark and doubtful presentiment...so ancient is the desire of one another which is implanted within us, reuniting our original nature, making one of two, and healing the state of man .

Plato

Hugging, kissing and flirting carry with them a certain frisson of sex. So! What's wrong with that? No matter how old we grow, we do not cease being sexual, even if we are not sexually active. Acknowledging our sexual selves, rejoicing in our sexuality and exercising it in all the ways possible to us is a very important part of our staying young as the years roll on.

Experts say that sex is a lifelong need and

that many older people remain sexually active. A person's level of sexual activity depends on a person's level of health and whether they are in a sexual partnership. Sexual activity is seen as being part of overall intimacy not just penetrative sex as all people have a need for warmth and sensual contact. From time to time you hear of people in their eighties finding love and experiencing the same passion they had when they were young. The heart is ageless and anyone at any age can fall in love. There is no age limit on sexuality. Most men and women between 50 and 80 are still enthusiastic about sex and intimacy. Use it or lose it! It is an ingredient that helps keep you active and alive.

Well, for some of us falling in love may be an option, for others it may be the continuation of a long-standing love.

The fires of love and youthful love may die down over the years, but maybe then it's time to revive them.

Successful relationships help to provide the fuel to staying young growing old. When people are supported and loved they tend to be happier and healthier than those who are isolated and alone. The more social contacts a person has also has a bearing on living a longer life. There was a gentleman aged 101 who lunched every day at the club and had a drink with his lady friend. Another 96 year old would regularly take out a couple of religious sisters to dine with him.

The message to you then, is that staying young, being young, thinking young and acting young while growing old calls for an acceptance, a recognition, an expression and a fostering of our continuing sexuality. If you are in a sexual relationship then keep that relationship alive and lively by making sure that sexual activity remains an element in the relationship. If you are not sexually partnered, still keep your sexuality as an element, where it is appropriate to do so, in your valued relationships. Don't be the classic old maid who mutters "I'm too old for that sort of thing".

Whenever you hear any older person claiming that they are well past sex think of the story of the young monk plagued by sexual temptations. In the middle of a restless night he runs from his cell to bang on the door of the oldest monk in the community, one who has lived the monastic life for nearly seventy years. "Brother, brother", the young monk cries, "how old will I be before these temptations cease?" "I don't know", is the reply. "Come back in ten years time and I might be able to tell you then!".

No one is ever well past sex. If they are, they are not just old, they're dead!

So, there it is. Staying young growing old. The essential message is that we do not treat each day as though it were to be our last. On the contrary each day is a beginning, an opportunity for new learnings, for setting challenges, for starting journeys, to awaken again the fearlessness of our youth. Obviously staying young through our senior years calls for some effort on our part. It also calls for planning. Many of us make a habit of noting each evening the things we propose to achieve the next day. At the end of the day, then, we can cross out those we succeeded in doing and relist the tasks for the next day. Nor need we limit our 'to do' lists to each day. We can plan the week ahead, the coming month and set timetables for what we are going to do next. Time isn't your enemy. You will need to manage your time well, but there is time to start whatever you set yourself to do. And remember that to run a marathon you have to take that first step, and keep running.

7. REFERENCES

Carnegie, Dale *How to Win Friends and Influence People.* Paperback edition. Sydney, Angus & Robertson, 1989.

Carroll, Lewis *Alice's Adventures in Wonderland.* London, Macmillan, 1988.

Chopra, Deepak *Ageless Body, Timeless Mind: Practical Alternative to Growing Old.* London, Rider, 1993.

Glover, John *Sydney Morning Herald.*

Keating, Kathleen *The Tiny Book of Hugs.* London, Fontana, 1992.

Macneice, Louis "Bagpipe Music" in www.poemhunter.com

Marquis, Don *Archy and Mehitabel.* Anchor, 1987.

Rohn, Jim *Seven Strategies for Wealth and Happiness.* Melbourne, Brolga, 1994.

ABOUT THE AUTHOR

Marji Hill is a well known Australian author who has specialised in writing books about all aspects of Australian Indigenous culture. Since she started producing books in 1976 she has co-authored more than sixty titles mainly for use in schools. In 1988 she produced a work of non-fiction *Six Australian Battlefields* which was published by Angus & Robertson. A decade later Allen & Unwin published a paperback edition. Marji's latest book *Staying Young Growing Old* represents a departure from her usual subject matter. For many years one of her passions has been studies in personal development. Marji lives on Queensland's Gold Coast in Australia where she works on writing new books and pursuing a career as an artist.